Bible Readers Series

A Study of Ephesians

MADE NEW THROUGH CHRIST

Jerald H. Jackson

Abingdon Press / Nashville

MADE NEW THROUGH CHRIST
A STUDY OF EPHESIANS

Copyright © 1993 by Cokesbury.
Abingdon Press edition published 2004.

Scripture quotations in this publication, unless otherwise indicated, are from the New Revised Standard Version of the Bible, copyrighted © 1989 by the Division of Christian Education of the National Council of the Churches of Christ in the United States of America, and are used by permission.

Lessons are based on the International Sunday School Lessons for Christian Teaching, copyright © 1989, by the Committee on the Uniform Series. Text excerpted from *Adult Bible Studies,* Summer 1993.

This book is printed on acid-free, elemental chlorine-free paper.

ISBN 978-0-687-03661-5

08 09 10 11 12 13—10 9 8 7 6 5 4 3
Manufactured in the United States of America.

CONTENTS

Chapter One

NEW LIFE

PURPOSE
To help us develop an understanding of the grace by which
God gives us the opportunity for faith

BIBLE PASSAGE
Ephesians 2:1-10

1 You were dead through the trespasses and sins   2 in
which you once lived, following the course of this world, following the ruler of the power of the air, the spirit that is now
at work among those who are disobedient.   3 All of us
once lived among them in the passions of our flesh, following the desires of flesh and senses, and we were by nature
children of wrath, like everyone else.   4 But God, who is
rich in mercy, out of the great love with which he loved us
5 even when we were dead through our trespasses, made
us alive together with Christ—by grace you have been
saved—   6 and raised us up with him and seated us with
him in the heavenly places in Christ Jesus,   7 so that in the
ages to come he might show the immeasurable riches of his
grace in kindness toward us in Christ Jesus.   8 For by grace
you have been saved through faith, and this is not your own
doing; it is the gift of God—   9 not the result of works, so

that no one may boast.   10 For we are what he has made us, created in Christ Jesus for good works, which God prepared beforehand to be our way of life.

Ephesians 3:14-19
14 For this reason I bow my knees before the Father, 15 from whom every family in heaven and on earth takes its name.   16 I pray that, according to the riches of his glory, he may grant that you may be strengthened in your inner being with power through his Spirit,   17 and that Christ may dwell in your hearts through faith, as you are being rooted and grounded in love.   18 I pray that you may have the power to comprehend, with all the saints, what is the breadth and length and height and depth,   19 and to know the love of Christ that surpasses knowledge, so that you may be filled with all the fullness of God.

CORE VERSE
By grace you have been saved through faith, and this is not your own doing; it is the gift of God. (Ephesians 2:8)

OUR NEED
I do not remember a time when the church was not an important part of my life. Of course, my father was a Methodist pastor—that helped. By the time my younger brother came along, we were known as the "Jackson eight." We usually filled a pew all by ourselves. The first songs I learned were hymns. The first friends I made were Sunday school chums. The first words I memorized were Scripture verses. The first ideas I encountered were religious ideas.

One of the hymns I learned was "Amazing Grace." It was a wonderful hymn to sing, but as a child I never quite understood the "I once was lost" part. Growing up in the church, I had always felt "found."

Eventually, I sought independence from my family and my church. After experiencing that part of faith's journey, which is best described as the absence of faith, I learned to make the faith my own. Only then did I understand the grace by which God gives the opportunity for faith; only then did I understand the meaning of the hymn:

> I once was lost,
>   but now am found;
> was blind, but now I see.[1]

FAITHFUL LIVING

The Christian experience begins with change. One way to understand this change is in terms of levels. On the higher level, a person lives for the realization of God's purposes. On the lower level, a person ignores God and lives for the fulfillment of his or her own purposes. In the opening verses of Ephesians 2, Paul describes those who live on the lower level, those who live in opposition to God.

Paul had lived on this level, as had the people to whom he wrote. They had once been loyal to "this world, following the ruler of the power of the air" (Ephesians 2:2); they had once been separated from God through disobedience and sin. During this time their lives had been based on self-interest and other destructive affections. They were, Paul said, "children of wrath" (Ephesians 2:3).

Occasionally, I hear Christians say that the word *wrath* is an Old Testament word that has no place in Christian thinking. Wrath was an important idea for Paul, however; and it should be for us. In his letter to the Romans, he wrote, "For the wrath of God is revealed from heaven against all ungodliness and wickedness of those who by their wickedness suppress the truth" (Romans 1:18). The wrath of God is quite simply the present and future consequence of humankind's disobedience.

"For those who are self-seeking and who obey not the truth

but wickedness, there will be wrath and fury" (Romans 2:8). In this verse the emphasis is on a future judgment. For Paul, life in sin was also a present judgment, however.

Most of us try to emphasize the positive things in life. Dwelling on life's problems can have a negative effect on our spirits. For example, my wife and I once spent an evening talking with some friends. The conversation turned to some of the disturbing things that had happened of late in our community. Each of us contributed our share to the message of gloom. Finally, a high school teacher began to tell us of the problems the schools in our community were having with young people carrying weapons. Two students had been shot dead; teachers were being intimidated by gangs; the schools were in chaos. Returning home later, we felt totally depressed about the state of our little corner of the world.

How else can we describe this situation other than by saying that we live in a world that is disobeying God and thus is experiencing the wrath of God? It seems that God has, in Paul's words, given us up to the "lusts of [our] hearts" (Romans 1:24).

Such conditions are not new. From what we know of human history, selfishness and wickedness have always been major forces in human life. Think of Paul's time and of those young churches in Asia Minor. One historian has said of Paul, Timothy, and other evangelists, "They went about establishing little communities of Christians among the Greeks and Romans, like men lighting lamps on dark streets at night."[2]

For Christians the motivation for faith has never been found in the goodness of humankind or in the pleasantness of life or in the ease with which the gospel is accepted. In our time there are many "dark streets," many people who are lost, many "children of wrath." The world is longing for "lamplighters" to speak of the possibilities of faith.

What does the phrase "children of wrath" mean to you?

Created for Good Works

When I first left the Midwest for the Southwest, I experienced a certain uneasiness. Among other things, I wondered, *What will the churches be like?*

You can tell a great deal about a congregation by noticing how the church is maintained and by reading the notices on the church bulletin boards. Using this standard, I have found that the church is an important part of life in all the communities of what at the time was my new area. Buildings are kept clean and serviceable. Members express a genuine concern for one another. Congregations are actively involved in meeting the needs of the immediate community and in reaching out in mission. These are people who believe and who care. They are living out the destiny Paul described: "For we are what he has made us, created in Christ Jesus for good works, which God prepared beforehand to be our way of life" (Ephesians 2:10).

Throughout the ages Christians have had the temptation to reverse the order of these things. We have been tempted to believe that God has chosen us because we are good rather than that God has chosen us to be good. The issue is as old as the church itself, as the Letter to the Ephesians attests. Paul reminded his readers, "For by grace you have been saved through faith, and this is not your own doing; it is the gift of God—not the result of works" (Ephesians 2:8-9).

Sometimes we are tempted to think that this sort of distinction is mere theological quibbling. Our reading of Scripture and of church history tells us that the order of grace and works is of fundamental importance, however. The spiritual truth is captured in Jesus' story of the Pharisee and the tax collector who went to the Temple to pray (Luke 18:9-14). The Pharisee thanked God that he was "not like other people: thieves, rogues, adulterers, or even like this tax collector" (Luke 18:11). The tax collector "would not even look up to heaven" but prayed, "God, be merciful to me, a sinner!"

(Luke 18:13). Jesus said that the tax collector "went down to his home justified rather than the other" (Luke 18:14).

"Justification by faith" is the great principle on which the Protestant church was founded. When Martin Luther and other leaders of the Reformation challenged the church of their day to give greater emphasis to God's grace, they found support in Paul's letters: "For we hold that a person is justified by faith apart from works prescribed by the law" (Romans 3:28).

Paul knew that people want to take an active role in determining their own lives, but he had seen how men and women can turn the gifts of God into destructive powers. Until we are united with God through Christ, our efforts or works are misdirected and futile. God loves us even though we do not and cannot earn that love: "God proves his love for us in that while we still were sinners Christ died for us" (Romans 5:8). God's grace creates the opportunity for good works, filling us with the fullness of God so that we can take up the way of life God intends for us.

How has the grace of God enabled you to do good works?

Filled With All the Fullness of God

What a beautiful prayer Paul offered in Ephesians 3:14-19! It is a heartfelt petition on behalf of the church Paul served and loved. It is also an inspiring reminder of the opportunities made possible for the Christian community through the indwelling Spirit of Christ.

The inspired community of faith believes that God has called the community together for a special purpose and that God will provide the resources required to perform the task. Filled with the fullness of God, we who are the church will be able to "accomplish abundantly far more than all we can ask or imagine" (Ephesians 3:20).

Some mainline denominations have been losing members in recent years. This decrease in membership has caused great consternation among clergy and laity alike. Much soul searching and self-criticism have taken place in church publications. The basic question seems to be, "What are we doing wrong?"

Seldom, however, has there been any suggestion that the membership decline might reflect the fact that the gospel does not always find receptive spirits. If, as some who analyze our culture say, we are passing through an era of unusual self-interest and greed, it should not be surprising that a gospel of selflessness and love would find hard, dry soil.

It seems to me that the proper question is not, "Is our church growing?" Rather, the proper question is, "Are we being faithful to the gospel?" Some of the issues that question raises for me are: Are we a forgiving fellowship? Do we honor everyone as a person of worth regardless of race, nationality, social standing, or sexual orientation? Do we express a lively and generous concern for the needy of the world? Does our witness show that we truly believe we are stewards of a world that belongs to God? Or, to use Paul's language, are we filled with all the fullness of God?

There is a strong temptation to believe that God's grace offers protection against the disasters and accidents of life. That belief is wrong. God's grace does not so much save us from life's troubles as it enables us to meet them with strength, courage, and hope. Grace gives us the power to respond to darkness with light, to evil with goodness, to indifference or hate with love, to need with charity, and to anger with understanding. In short, grace gives us opportunity for faith, for being the church.

How has your church experienced the power of God's grace in meeting the challenges of your life together?

CLOSING PRAYER

Almighty God, our very present help in trouble, encourage us with the sense of your presence in our church. Strengthen us for the tasks that are ours, and help us to live on the high level of your purposes. In Jesus' name we pray. Amen.

[1]From "Amazing Grace," in *The United Methodist Hymnal* (Copyright © 1989 by The United Methodist Publishing House); 378.
[2]From *The Interpreter's Bible,* Volume VII (Abingdon-Cokesbury Press, 1951); page 81.

Chapter Two

NEW FELLOWSHIP

PURPOSE
To help us recognize that the church is called to be an inclusive community that God has established through Jesus Christ

BIBLE PASSAGE
Ephesians 2:11-22

11 So then, remember that at one time you Gentiles by birth, called "the uncircumcision" by those who are called "the circumcision"—a physical circumcision made in the flesh by human hands— 12 remember that you were at that time without Christ, being aliens from the commonwealth of Israel, and strangers to the covenants of promise, having no hope and without God in the world. 13 But now in Christ Jesus you who once were far off have been brought near by the blood of Christ. 14 For he is our peace; in his flesh he has made both groups into one and has broken down the dividing wall, that is, the hostility between us. 15 He has abolished the law with its commandments and ordinances, that he might create in himself one new humanity in place of the two, thus making peace, 16 and might reconcile both groups to God in one body through the cross,

thus putting to death that hostility through it.   17 So he came and proclaimed peace to you who were far off and peace to those who were near;   18 for through him both of us have access in one Spirit to the Father.   19 So then you are no longer strangers and aliens, but you are citizens with the saints and also members of the household of God, 20 built upon the foundation of the apostles and prophets, with Christ Jesus himself as the cornerstone.   21 In him the whole structure is joined together and grows into a holy temple in the Lord;   22 in whom you also are built together spiritually into a dwelling place for God.

CORE VERSE
You are no longer strangers and aliens, but you are citizens with the saints and also members of the household of God.
(Ephesians 2:19)

OUR NEED

Every congregation I have served as pastor has been something of a spiritual mystery. I have often wondered why, in God's wisdom, just these particular people have gathered here at just this particular time. Is our being together merely the result of a series of coincidences?

Considering a congregation in my mind's eye, I see a remarkable variety of people. On this side is a young family. They probably had difficulty getting everyone ready on time, but somehow they managed. In front of them is an eighty-year-old widow who, as is her custom, walked the ten blocks from her home to be at worship. On the right is a successful businesswoman who traveled all week. She easily could have justified spending Sunday morning at home. In the same pew is a surgeon who put in a seventy-hour week. Sitting near the back is a family struggling financially and emotionally, with two children in college and four aging parents needing their support. All these people and others have gathered as this one church to praise God and to seek God's guidance for their lives.

In this chapter we will consider Paul's understanding of the church as a new expression of God's creative power. Being the church, people of all races and stations experience new life as children of their heavenly Parent. Each gains access to this community through the forgiving love of God, and each is called in turn to play an active part in the forgiving community.

FAITHFUL LIVING

Paul felt God had called him to proclaim Christ "among the Gentiles" (Galatians 1:16; Ephesians 3:2-6), and he had been remarkably successful in doing so. Thus by the time the Letter to the Ephesians was written, a substantial portion of the church was Gentile—that is, non-Jewish—in origin.

Acts 15 tells of Paul's struggle with the Jerusalem Christians over the inclusion of Gentiles in the church. Eventually, Gentiles were allowed to become part of the church without undergoing or observing Jewish rites. Paul was convinced that God was creating a new inclusive community through the life, death, and resurrection of Jesus Christ.

One of the images Paul used to describe this new community was that of "household." To the Gentile Christians he wrote, "You are ... members of the household of God" (Ephesians 2:19). Paul contrasted this newfound status with the Gentiles' former condition in which they had "no hope" and were "without God in the world" (Ephesians 2:12).

Hope was a basic ingredient of Christian faith for Paul. The Christian can hope because God has been victorious over the ancient enemies of humankind: sin and death. Paul described this victory in his first letter to the Corinthians, Chapter 15. The resurrection of Christ is the first evidence of God's victory. Then, upon Christ's return, "those who belong to Christ" will be raised (1 Corinthians 15:23). So Paul concluded that Christians need not grieve "as others do who have no hope" over those who have died (1 Thessalonians 4:13). The church, the new inclusive community, has a common hope.

In your experience, how is the church different from other communities or organizations?

A Place in the World

How plaintive is Paul's description of the Gentiles before God's act in Christ: "You were ... strangers to the covenants of promise, having no hope and without God in the world" (Ephesians 2:12). Paul respected the special relationship between God and the people of Israel. Among the covenants of promise to which he referred were those given to Abraham (Genesis 15:1-21; 17:1-22), Moses (Exodus 24:1-11), Isaiah (Isaiah 55:3), and Jeremiah (Jeremiah 31:31-34). The Gentiles, not having been blessed with these covenants, were "without God in the world" (Ephesians 2:12)—a powerful definition of what the feeling of homelessness must be like.

Most of us have an idea of "home," made up of our better experiences or dreams. Home is our place of safety. It provides shelter from weather and other dangers. It is a place where we can be ourselves, where we can "let down our hair," as the saying goes. Home is a place of rest and healing, a place we can find temporary relief from the stresses of life. No wonder we are concerned about homeless persons: Without a home, where does one turn to find safety, love, acceptance, nourishment, healing, and encouragement?

Of course, home is also a place where we experience responsibility and where we learn the rules of behavior. Paul used this familiar idea to convey the notion of the church. To be sure, the makeup of the average home in Paul's time would have been quite different from what we know today. As one student of the period said, "An ancient household, of course, included a man's slaves, hired servants and dependent relatives, as well as children; it might be quite a large establishment."[1] The basic human needs that a home provides have remained largely the same throughout history, however. Paul's point was that the Gentiles and the Jews had been given a home together by the act of God in Jesus Christ.

Paul spoke of God as "Father." The idea of Father conveyed an important and easily understood truth about God in the period during which the letters were written. Being father of a family brought responsibility and authority. In this passage, Paul stressed that God is the Father of both Jew and Gentile, providing a home, a place in the world, for both.

How does being a Christian give you a sense of having a place in the world?

A Wall Broken Down

Being an "outsider" is not a comfortable feeling. I recall traveling in a foreign country where I did not know the language. I had a strong sense of alienation and separation. Some people experience this feeling even when language is not a problem, for many other barriers can separate us from one another. In this portion of the Letter to the Ephesians, we see Paul celebrating the crumbling of a great barrier between Gentile and Jew.

Paul described a view in which the world was divided into Jews on the one hand and Gentiles on the other. Jews considered Gentiles to be "unclean." Male Gentiles were not circumcised. They did not participate in the prescribed purification rites. Therefore the especially holy parts of the Temple were not open to them. A wall in the Temple separated the court of Israel from the court of the Gentiles (Ephesians 2:14).

Francis W. Beare, in his exegesis of Ephesians in *The Interpreter's Bible,* wrote that during an archaeological excavation of the Temple sites in 1871, a piece of the dividing wall was discovered. The fragment contained this warning: "No man of another race is to proceed within the partition and enclosing wall about the sanctuary; and anyone arrested there will have himself to blame for the penalty of death which will be imposed as a consequence."[2] The inscription was written in Greek.

Paul seized the idea of the dividing wall and used it to explain the new community created in Christ. This new community is possible because God has changed the situation for both Jew and Gentile. For the Jew, God has "abolished the law with its commandments and ordinances" (Ephesians 2:15). For the Gentile, God has ended the alienation that left the Gentiles "far off" (Ephesians 2:13). Now both have a new opportunity to love and serve God as one people; for God has created "in himself one new humanity in place of the two, thus making peace" (Ephesians 2:15). God invites both Gentile and Jew into the new household that is no longer divided. In the name of Jesus Christ, "our peace" (Ephesians 2:14), Gentile and Jew can come together before God.

Christians have struggled throughout history to live out the new humanity that Paul envisioned as coming together in inclusive congregations. While our churches do contain persons of many ages, races, and stations in life, the attainment of "one body" (Ephesians 2:16) continues to elude us. Perhaps this is the case because we have not yet taken with absolute seriousness the fact that God is the divine Parent in the newly created household. If God is head of the household, God's rules must prevail. Since God created the church through forgiveness, the members of the church are called upon to be the forgiving community.

A fellowship based on the forgiving love of God must never forget its origins. True, in the early days of the church, the Jewish Christians sought to exclude others, treating some Christians as outsiders. If history teaches us anything, however, it is that every group has separatist tendencies and tries to build a wall between people. Remember, for example, the Puritans who fled England in the sixteenth century to find religious freedom. Within a few years they were denying that same freedom to others. It may be that when Paul reminded the Gentiles that they were once "aliens" and "strangers," he did so to counter a growing feeling of self-satisfaction in the Gentile church.

In our own experience we know that it is easy to become comfortable in the church and to look askance at persons who seem to be different from us. One of the churches I served as pastor was especially "family oriented." In fact, it was so "family oriented" that the occasional single person who came to that church found little opportunity to become active. Some single persons confided to me that they did not feel particularly welcome. They saw themselves as outsiders.

We must remember that the church is a place where walls are broken down. That is why those of us who are Gentiles were accepted, and that is why we must help others to feel included.

Did you ever feel like an outsider in the church? If so, who helped you overcome that feeling?

A Dwelling Place for God

We often speak of the church building as God's house. Nothing could be further from the truth. When Paul wrote that Christians are "built together spiritually into a dwelling place for God" (Ephesians 2:22), there were no church buildings as we know them. Christians gathered in private homes for worship. Paul's image of church included neither steeples nor pews. Paul wrote of a flesh and blood institution made up of women, men, and children whose lives had been graced by the presence of Jesus Christ.

For me, the spiritual community of which Paul wrote is most visible when United Methodists gather for annual conferences. Our "oneness in Christ" obscures the fact that we come together from many different backgrounds and places. In my conference, we exhibit a wonderful variety: rural, urban, Anglo, Native American, Hispanic, African American, and Asian. Also, the people hold a significant variety of theological perspectives. Annual conference helps us maintain the vision of the church as one great household, the dwelling place of God.

It is astonishing to realize that centuries ago, long before the modern achievements in travel and communication, Paul set out from Antioch to preach in Asia Minor, then on to Greece, then on to Rome; and he even had his eye on Spain. As large as the world must have seemed to him, it was not too large for the gospel of Jesus Christ. Paul knew that God had chosen to "gather up all things in [Christ]" (Ephesians 1:10), ending the hostility and "thus making peace" (Ephesians 2:15).

If true peace is ever to be achieved, it will be built on the basis that Paul described, the basis of one great household. John Wesley, founder of Methodism, urged inclusiveness in the church. He based his sermon "Catholic Spirit" on a text from 2 Kings 10:15: "Is your heart as true to mine as mine is to yours?... If it is, give me your hand." Wesley wrote, "But although a difference in opinions or modes of worship may prevent an entire external union, yet need it prevent our union in affection? Though we can't think alike, may we not love alike?"[3] This statement captures the essence of the inclusive community founded upon Jesus Christ, the community that is a dwelling place for God.

How has your Christian faith enabled you to accept persons who differ from you?

> **CLOSING PRAYER**
>
> **Almighty God, who through Jesus has brought us a renewed vision of peace, strengthen us through your Spirit that we may receive all your children as brothers and sisters in Christ. In Jesus' name we pray. Amen.**

[1] From *An Introduction to the Theology of the New Testament,* by Alan Richardson (Harper & Brothers, Publishers, 1958); page 263.

[2] From *The Interpreter's Bible,* Volume X (Abingdon-Cokesbury Press, 1951); page 655.

[3] From *The Works of John Wesley,* Volume 2, edited by Albert C. Outler (Abingdon Press, 1985); page 82.

Chapter Three

NEW BEHAVIOR

PURPOSE

To help us examine our lives and consider how they can be pleasing to the Lord

BIBLE PASSAGE

Ephesians 5:1-20

1 Be imitators of God, as beloved children, 2 and live in love, as Christ loved us and gave himself up for us, a fragrant offering and sacrifice to God.

3 But fornication and impurity of any kind, or greed, must not even be mentioned among you, as is proper among saints. 4 Entirely out of place is obscene, silly, and vulgar talk; but instead, let there be thanksgiving. 5 Be sure of this, that no fornicator or impure person, or one who is greedy (that is, an idolater), has any inheritance in the kingdom of Christ and of God.

6 Let no one deceive you with empty words, for because of these things the wrath of God comes on those who are disobedient. 7 Therefore do not be associated with them. 8 For once you were darkness, but now in the Lord you are light. Live as children of light— 9 for the fruit of the light is found in all that is good and right and true. 10 Try to

find out what is pleasing to the Lord.   11 Take no part in the unfruitful works of darkness, but instead expose them. 12 For it is shameful even to mention what such people do secretly;   13 but everything exposed by the light becomes visible,   14 for everything that becomes visible is light. Therefore it says,

> "Sleeper awake!
> Rise from the dead,
> and Christ will shine on you."

15 Be careful then how you live, not as unwise people but as wise,   16 making the most of the time, because the days are evil.   17 So do not be foolish, but understand what the will of the Lord is.   18 Do not get drunk with wine, for that is debauchery; but be filled with the Spirit, 19 as you sing psalms and hymns and spiritual songs among yourselves, singing and making melody to the Lord in your hearts,   20 giving thanks to God the Father at all times and for everything in the name of our Lord Jesus Christ.

CORE VERSES

Be imitators of God, as beloved children, and live in love, as Christ loved us and gave himself up for us. (Ephesians 5:1-2)

OUR NEED

At some point in my high school days, I read a biography of Thomas Alva Edison. I remember being impressed, not so much by his many inventions, as by the fact that Edison managed to get by on only four hours of sleep per night. For some reason I thought that was an ideal worth emulating. Yet, try as I might, I always seemed to require more sleep.

Later in life I learned of John Wesley's pattern of early rising. In his sermon "On Redeeming the Time," the founder of Methodism emphasized the importance of managing sleep. While he granted that each person would require a different amount of sleep, he suspected that the human tendency was to sleep more than nature required. He explained that early in his life, after a period of wakefulness, he began experimenting with sleep and discovered that he was best served if he rose every day at 4 A.M.[1]

Here was another ideal that challenged my sense of stewardship. Alas, I failed again. While the examples of great persons are intended to inspire us—and most of them do—the achievements of Wesley and Edison in this regard have always left me with feelings of inferiority.

In the Letter to the Ephesians, Paul takes us a step beyond the example of special persons. It is something of a shock to realize that he was urging Christians to imitate God (Ephesians 5:1). Isn't that too much to ask? How can we live lives pleasing to the Lord if we are expected to be perfect?

FAITHFUL LIVING

When I began my ordained ministry, I carried into it certain ideas about what the perfect pastor would be like. I thought that one aspect of pastoral perfection was the ability to remember names. (It was very flattering to have someone say, "Isn't it marvelous how he remembers all our names!") I thought myself quite good at remembering, taking pride in recalling the names of even the visiting relatives of a member. Then came my downfall.

Looking out over the congregation one Easter, I spied the mother of one of our members. I knew that she had visited from a distant town on the previous Christmas. I was primed and ready. When the service ended and the family passed by to greet me, I quickly said, "And it is so nice to see you again Mrs. London." With a sweet smile she looked at me and said softly, "It's *Berlin*." This comeuppance taught me two important lessons: A successful ministry is not founded on any sort of trick, and nobody is perfect.

Perfectionism can be a disabling attitude. I have known a few people over the years who were such perfectionists that they never completed any task, and I have known a few who were even unable to begin one. John Wesley's doctrine of perfection was roundly criticized in his own time, largely because it was nearly always misunderstood. In his sermon "On Perfection," Wesley defined this doctrine as the perfection of love: "This is the sum of Christian perfection: it is all comprised in that one word, love."[2]

Wesley did not justify his doctrine on any evidence that Christians had ever achieved perfection but on the fact that God promises it. "Nothing can be wanting on God's part. As he has called us to holiness he is undoubtedly willing, as well as able, to work this holiness in us. For he cannot mock his helpless creatures, calling us to receive what he never intends to give."[3]

Wesley chose to focus, not on the obvious failings of humankind, but on the promise of God. Wesley's faith in the power of God was stronger than his realistic appraisal of human behavior. The truth that inspired Wesley and the apostle Paul before him is still relevant to us. At issue is not whether we believe in ourselves but whether we believe in God and in the power of God to achieve the divine purpose.

What does the word* perfection *mean to you?

Temptations in Daily Life

If our lives are to be pleasing to the Lord, we must find the wisdom, strength, and courage to resist behavior that does not honor God. Such behavior is destructive of God's purpose for our lives. A friend of mine, who taught in a local business college, shared with me some of the frustrations she had when her students gave in to destructive behavior.

Because of the nature of the community in which the college was located, many of the students were from disadvantaged homes and had not finished high school. Of course, in a business school certain skills needed to be learned, such as typing, writing business letters, using calculators, and the like. What saddened and frustrated my friend was the students' vulnerability to the pressure of their peers regarding this necessary learning.

Some of the students had friends who ridiculed their efforts to improve themselves. Occasionally, that ridicule became so strong that a student dropped out of school. Others associated with people who abused alcohol and other drugs and were manipulated by their group to participate in this dangerous activity. My friend tried to help her students see that they must take responsibility for their own lives. She told them that by giving in to the group, they were forsaking their right of personal choice. They needed to know that they could resist.

One tactic my friend used was to say as frequently as the occasion allowed, "No one cares about you as much as you do yourself. If your so-called friends pressure you into damaging and destructive behavior or into behavior that will not allow you to fulfill your potential, what sort of 'friend' is that?" But it was difficult to win the debate. The students wanted to be accepted by their peer group, so they often behaved in ways they believed would please their group. It was hard to break free of the pressure.

Paul was aware of the sort of social pressure that resulted in negative behavior. That is why he so strongly advised Christians not to associate with "those who are disobedient" (Ephesians 5:6-7).

Our American culture sustains some negative values. The use of alcohol, for instance, continues to be accepted in spite of the statistics that prove it contributes to many fatalities on our highways, to lost employment, to spousal abuse, and to ruined families. Young people can be persuaded that it is "natural" and "human" to experiment with drugs because of what they see adults doing with alcohol.

It is not just peer group pressure or media influence that leads to destructive behavior. One day a young businessman, a member of our church, stopped by to visit. He was employed in a respected company and was a successful member of the management team. After a few minutes of pleasantries, he began to tell me how he was being pressured to manipulate the books of the company. His job was on the line if he did not cooperate. He was in deep anguish over the terrible choice he had to make.

If he refused, he would lose his job and subject his family to the economic uncertainties that were sure to follow. If he went along with the deception, he would deny his fundamental Christian ethic. As with all life's dilemmas, no one else could make the decision for him.

How has your faith helped you resolve a moral problem or reject a spiritually unhealthy influence?

An Ethic of Love

The Christian faith teaches an ethic based on love. Paul's objection to fornication, impurity, covetousness, and vulgarity (Ephesians 5:3-4) was based on the knowledge that these activities and dispositions dishonor God's intent for creation.

While it is a mistake to think that the only moral decisions facing early Christians were related to sex, the misuse of God's gift of sexuality was a great concern to Paul. New Testament scholars tell us that in the culture of first-century Asia Minor, there were those who believed that human physical and spiritual natures were separated. These persons taught that one's spiritual life was untouched by any sort of sexual practice.[4] This philosophy was entirely out of keeping with the central tenets of Christianity.

During my lifetime American culture has undergone what has been called a sexual revolution. Some people argued that the old taboos regarding sexuality needed to be cast off. They said that the repression of sexuality was evil.

In more recent years a new "conservatism" has arisen. Now the watchword has been changed from free sex to "safe" sex. Lost in all the discussion about the physical diseases that can be transmitted through casual sex is the spiritual dimension of human sexuality.

What happens to a person's spiritual life if his or her sexuality is abused? As Christians, we seek to understand ourselves, our needs of body, mind, and spirit, as part of God's good creation. We believe that our physical and spiritual natures are inseparable. We believe that if we use God's gifts as they were intended, we will find both personal and social fulfillment. Conversely, if we misuse them, God's purpose for us will be damaged and community life will be disrupted.

While it is important to give witness to moral behavior and to exhort Christians to high ethical standards, it is imperative that such a witness not be judgmental but rather be redemptive. To put it bluntly, it is not helpful simply to preach that "sinners" will "go to hell"; rather, we should preach that sinners can be saved.

Too often, Christians have been seen as expressing a "holier than thou" attitude that shuts out persons who could benefit from a wholesome fellowship. Thankfully, many congregations are now reaching out to persons who have experienced the tragic consequences of casual sex. Our central witness should be our experience of the redemptive power of God in our own lives and our belief that God extends redemption to all persons.

How does an ethic of love allow us to take a stand against immorality without being judgmental?

Fellowship and Faithfulness

Paul placed a strong emphasis on the importance of the Christian community and the power for wholesome living it provided. We have seen how alert he was to the dangerous negative influences of non-Christian culture. He was even more sure of the positive influence that the healthy Christian community provided for its members. Thus, writing on living a life pleasing to the Lord, Paul counseled Christians to use the psalms and songs of faith within the fellowship (Ephesians 5:18-20).

I think such advice comes from Paul's certainty that participation in the Christian fellowship is crucial to individual faithfulness. We need to have the support of others who are also determined to live in a way that pleases and honors God. Christians are called to new behavior—a behavior that is modeled on the spirit of Christ.

Certainly, this is why churches have supported the Sunday school movement. We have understood the importance of providing positive environments for children and adults. It is no accident that in the sacrament of baptism, after the parents and sponsors make their promises to God, the members of the congregation are asked to affirm their part in the spiritual development of the child.

There is much discussion these days about the fact that legally we can neither teach religion nor offer prayer in the public schools. Some argue that this situation has a damaging effect on the lives of children, and they may have a point. Yet, if the church took with complete seriousness our responsibility for providing the right spiritual environment for our children and displayed the commitment to our children that would draw the interest of parents outside our walls, then the absence of prayer or religion in the public schools would be of little consequence.

How has Christian fellowship strengthened your resolve to live a life pleasing to the Lord?

CLOSING PRAYER
Almighty and loving God, inspire us by the promise of your gospel that we may ever seek to grow in grace and love and to express goodness in our daily lives. In the name of your Son, Jesus Christ our Lord, we pray. Amen.

[1] From *The Works of John Wesley,* Volume 3, edited by Albert C. Outler (Abingdon Press, 1986); page 325.
[2] From *The Works of John Wesley,* Volume 3; page 74.
[3] From *The Works of John Wesley,* Volume 3; page 77.
[4] From *The Interpreter's Bible,* Volume X (Abingdon-Cokesbury Press, 1953); pages 705–706.

Chapter Four

New Family Order

PURPOSE

To show how the general principle of mutual self-giving guides the Christian household

BIBLE PASSAGE

Ephesians 5:21-33

21 **Be subject to one another out of reverence for Christ.**

22 **Wives, be subject to your husbands as you are to the Lord.** 23 **For the husband is the head of the wife just as Christ is the head of the church, the body of which he is the Savior.** 24 **Just as the church is subject to Christ, so also wives ought to be, in everything, to their husbands.**

25 **Husbands, love your wives, just as Christ loved the church and gave himself up for her,** 26 **in order to make her holy by cleansing her with the washing of water by the word,** 27 **so as to present the church to himself in splendor, without a spot or wrinkle or anything of the kind—yes, so that she may be holy and without blemish.** 28 **In the same way, husbands should love their wives as they do their own bodies. He who loves his wife loves himself.** 29 **For no one ever hates his own body, but he nourishes and tenderly cares for it, just as Christ does for the church,**

31

30 because we are members of his body.   31 "For this reason a man will leave his father and mother and be joined to
his wife, and the two will become one flesh."   32 This is
a great mystery, and I am applying it to Christ and the
church.   33 Each of you, however, should love his wife as
himself, and a wife should respect her husband.

Ephesians 6:1-4
1 Children, obey your parents in the Lord, for this is
right.   2 "Honor your father and mother"—this is the first
commandment with a promise: 3 "so that it may be well
with you and you may live long on the earth."

4 And, fathers, do not provoke your children to anger,
but bring them up in the discipline and instruction of the
Lord.

CORE VERSE

Be subject to one another out of reverence for Christ.
(Ephesians 5:21)

OUR NEED

In our times, families live under intense pressure. The
stress on marriage and child rearing is taking its toll. Some
say that the traditional family structure is becoming a thing
of the past.

Marriage, one of the most basic of our social institutions,
is enduring severe shocks. Most of us would agree that laws
allowing people to be freed from relationships that severely
damage and constrain them are a good thing. Across the
broad sweep of American culture, however, marriage seems
to be treated as a quaint artifact of a bygone era. Like most
other "products" of our time, marriage has become dispos-
able. If it "wears out," we just throw it away.

The number of single persons rearing children has grown dramatically as a result. These families are usually headed by a woman, and many of them live in poverty. Yet, even when there are two parents in the family, economic demands often require both to be employed, adding to the strain on family life.

My office is situated next to a day care center. Most of the children spend ten-to-twelve hours at the center each weekday. While the care the children receive is excellent, they are experiencing a different form of family life than many of us have known.

In this chapter we see how Paul tried to address the everyday problems Christian families faced in his time. In particular, we will consider how the relationship between husband and wife and between parent and child can be informed by the gospel of Jesus Christ.

FAITHFUL LIVING

As a pastor I often used the lectionary as a source for preaching texts. Using the lectionary protected me from relying too frequently on my favorite passages. It ensured that the congregation, over a period of years, would be exposed to the full scope of the Scriptures. Such a practice can have its awkward moments, however.

I recall one occasion when an associate, who was scheduled to preach, refused to use the assigned epistle reading because it included the verse in which Paul said that women should be silent in the church (1 Corinthians 14:33-35). This message offended his understanding of the new status of women created by the gospel of Jesus Christ. Today, the thought that women should be silent in the church is both shocking and unacceptable. Some of our most able church leaders and preachers are women.

Yet we should recognize the context of Paul's statement. Paul was concerned to interpret the gospel for the social situation of his day. What is truly remarkable is that Paul was able to reorder social values as much as he did. His teachings on marriage and family life show that Paul wanted to bring the love of God expressed in Jesus Christ to bear on all human relationships. Just as God's act in Christ restored the image of God in the individual, so it could transform the relationship between husband and wife, parent and child. The family could be a model of God's love for the world.

How do you think Christian faith can enrich family relationships?

True Companions

In my mind's eye I still see the event clearly. I was in my first pastorate, very young and very inexperienced. The young couple who sat before me planning their wedding presented me with a strange request. As we proceeded through our discussion of the marriage service and the vows they would be taking, the young woman said, "Please put the words *and obey* in my vows."

I explained that the vows written for the marriage service were carefully chosen to reflect the understanding that each person comes to the marriage relationship as an equal. Really, nothing more was needed. The vows were quite complete. She insisted. "No," she said, "I want to promise that I will love, honor, cherish, and obey my husband."

As pastors know, there comes a point in such discussions when there is no more room for rational negotiation. I gave in. I performed the wedding service just as the bride had requested.

Within six months the marriage was over. The bride who had promised to obey her husband had walked out of the marriage. It was my first lesson in the long process of learning that words alone do not make relationships.

The vow of obedience to a husband is troubling to many Christians, for Christian marriage should be based on mutual self-giving. Each partner should honor the other's dignity and individuality. Paul said this explicitly: "Be subject to one another out of reverence for Christ" (Ephesians 5:21). His counsel on marriage between Christians was a radical rethinking of the ideas current in his first-century culture. Christians were searching for new principles upon which to build the Christian family. They were not content with the old answers, either pagan or Jewish.

Mutual self-giving or subjection is both the glory and the agony of Christian marriage. Much simpler would be a relationship in which one partner totally submits to the other, no questions asked. Much simpler, yes, but with no chance of creating the fulfillment that God intended for marriage.

We read of that intent in the Scriptures: "For this reason a man will leave his father and mother and be joined to his wife, and the two will become one flesh" (Ephesians 5:31; see Genesis 2:24). The Genesis account of Creation reminds us that

> God created humankind in
> his image,
> in the image of God he created
> them;
> male and female he created
> them.
> (Genesis 1:27)

In our culture we have for so long thought of God in masculine terms that we have to struggle to remember that both male and female are created in God's image. The woman is no less the image of God, the man, no more. Or, to put it another way, neither sex alone fulfills the image of God. It is in becoming "one flesh," in becoming true companions, that such a fulfillment is realized.

This is the challenge of every marriage. We should never lose our individual personalities; but we should strive to become true companions, to cherish the uniqueness of the other. Of course, doing so can be difficult. In every person there are those little habits that the other partner "endures" for the sake of harmony. Yet sometimes in a moment of insight, we discover that it is precisely those expressive quirks that endear the other to us.

My wife has the habit of never completely closing a dresser drawer. During the first years of our marriage, whenever some stress or other would get to me, I would, with great flourish, slam shut all the partially open drawers, thinking, *Why can't she do a simple thing like shutting drawers?* Then a family emergency took my wife out of town for more than a week. After several days I noticed that there were no partially open drawers. Instead of feeling relieved, I was overcome with a longing for her presence. I realized how important to me the signs of her presence were. I have never shut a drawer since. Mutual self-giving begins in cherishing the other person for what he or she is.

Inevitably, there is a division of labor within a marriage. Duties and responsibilities are to be shared between the husband and wife so that "their home may be a haven of blessing and peace,"[1] as one marriage service describes.

My parents, now dead, enjoyed a long marriage. Over a lifetime together the division of labor in their relationship became quite established. When my father died, it was difficult for my mother to carry on alone. I recall phoning her several months after my father's death with the usual question, "How are you doing?" From between clenched teeth she said, "Well, I did something today I've never had to do before." "What's that, Mother?" I asked. She responded, "I changed a fuse!" In her reply she displayed an odd mixture of anger and pride: anger that she—after all these years—would have to do such a thing; pride that she was able to do it.

In my own marriage my wife has graciously put my vocation first. I have been grateful that she was willing to allow my vocation to determine where we would live and for how long. It always meant that she left special friends and job opportunities behind. As I neared retirement, we agreed that she would choose where we would live. As Paul said, "Be subject to one another" (Ephesians 2:21).

As I look at younger couples, I realize that they have an even more difficult task in being mutually self-giving. Careers are no longer the province of husbands only. Child rearing does not necessarily fall on the mother alone. Social structures change, and the modern family must negotiate a new set of rules to become true companions. The principle Paul set forth endures, however: Christian marriage is to be nurtured by mutual self-giving.

What marriages with which you are familiar have been marked by Paul's principle of mutual self-giving?

Care and Discipline

On September 19, 1959, our first child was born. It was a breathtaking event. I can still recall many of the small details of the experience. How poorly prepared I was for the reality of having a third person in the family! I had thought of an infant as a docile, pliable being. I realized within a few days, however, that here was a person with a set of needs that did not conform to mine. What a shock to discover that our child had—from the very beginning—a mind and will of his own.

I now realize that those early years were relatively simple compared with what came later. Small children do usually respond cooperatively to the needs of the larger family. The real challenge comes when the inner development of the child requires that he or she assert independence from the family. This need is amplified by the growing desire to be accepted by a peer group—usually at the expense of family values. All parents, of course, have been adolescents too; but most of us are not prepared when our first child becomes one.

Paul counseled obedience from children and careful parenting from fathers. (Naturally, we would add mothers as well.) His advice was, "Do not provoke your children to anger, but bring them up in the discipline and instruction of the Lord" (Ephesians 6:4).

Knowing comes from learning, and learning comes from experience. Every generation needs to learn some of the simple lessons all over again. To bring children up in the discipline and instruction of the Lord, Christian parents should first remember what the Lord has done in their lives, how the Lord has carefully, patiently, lovingly tended to them. If Paul counseled Christians to "be kind to one another, tenderhearted, forgiving one another, as God in Christ has forgiven you" (Ephesians 4:32), does this not also apply to the relationship of parent to child?

At times the inexperience of the young will lead them in the wrong direction. There was the time on Princess Street in Edinburgh, Scotland, when my wife and I suddenly realized that our five-year-old son had wandered off. A few frantic moments passed before we found him happily and innocently looking in a store window, unconcerned about it all. We were quite concerned, however. Parents must take active care, even intervening care, as their children grow.

Yet, there comes a time when that intervention is inappropriate. Parents must be ready to give up their protective role when the time is right. Our goal is not to keep our children dependent on us but to help them discover their own powers and to bring them into their own relationship with the Lord.

This goal involves awesome responsibility. I have known adults who found it difficult to think of God as "Father" or "Parent" because childhood and youth in their family was so disabling. For these injured people we hold out the hope that the mercy and love of God can redeem the tragedy of their unhappy childhood.

During our children's "difficult years," we found a sharing group within the church that provided us with support and information that helped us—and our children—through. Part of the church's contribution to our life together comes through such groups that help us bring up our children in the care and discipline of the Lord. Let us encourage one another to take advantage of these ministries of the church.

How can the church help support parents and bring children into a creative relationship with God?

CLOSING PRAYER
Gracious God, you have entrusted us with the tender relationships of family. Support us with your own spirit of love and concern that we may meet the needs of those closest to us. In the name of your Son we pray. Amen.

---

[1]From "A Service of Christian Marriage," in *The United Methodist Hymnal* (Copyright © 1989 by The United Methodist Publishing House); 864.

Chapter Five

NEW STRENGTH

PURPOSE

To help us recognize that truth, righteousness, peace, and faith are the armor that enables us to stand against the power of evil

BIBLE PASSAGE

Ephesians 6:10-20

10 **Be strong in the Lord and in the strength of his power. 11 Put on the whole armor of God, so that you may be able to stand against the wiles of the devil.   12 For our struggle is not against enemies of blood and flesh, but against the rulers, against the authorities, against the cosmic powers of this present darkness, against the spiritual forces of evil in the heavenly places.   13 Therefore take up the whole armor of God, so that you may be able to withstand on that evil day, and having done everything, to stand firm. 14 Stand therefore, and fasten the belt of truth around your waist, and put on the breastplate of righteousness.   15 As shoes for your feet put on whatever will make you ready to proclaim the gospel of peace.   16 With all of these, take the shield of faith, with which you will be able to quench all the flaming arrows of the evil one.   17 Take the helmet**

of salvation, and the sword of the Spirit, which is the word of God.

18 Pray in the Spirit at all times in every prayer and supplication. To that end keep alert and always persevere in supplication for all the saints. 19 Pray also for me, so that when I speak, a message may be given to me to make known with boldness the mystery of the gospel, 20 for which I am an ambassador in chains. Pray that I may declare it boldly, as I must speak.

CORE VERSE

Be strong in the Lord and in the strength of his power.
(Ephesians 6:10)

OUR NEED

Who among us does not wish that the world was a better place? Some young couples have shared with me their decision not to have children because the planet is in such a mess. Well, while those of us who are older may sympathize, I doubt we would want to try to prove life was substantially better fifty or one hundred years ago. Certainly, the world in which Jesus lived and died was deeply troubled. While the Scriptures state clearly that Jesus died at the "right time" (Romans 5:6), they also reveal that it was not a good time.

Thus, while we feel vulnerable to evil today, so did the Christians to whom Paul originally wrote. Paul knew that the strength of evil lies in its power to discourage and dishearten and that the intention of evil is to destroy faith. In this regard, times have not changed. For reasons that are hidden in the mind and purpose of God, evil continues to be a force against which we must contend. The gospel of Jesus Christ provides resources we can use in the struggle of faith, however. The Letter to the Ephesians is especially helpful in this regard.

Nowhere is Christian hope more eloquently expressed than in the last section of Ephesians. Paul knew the source of our hope. It is not the innate goodness of humankind or the general flow of the universe. We can be hopeful because our God is a great God. "Be strong in the Lord and in the strength of his power" (Ephesians 6:10), Paul urged. This was what he wanted Christians scattered in the little churches of Asia Minor and southern Europe to remember.

In this chapter we will see how Paul reminded the Ephesians of some resources that God has made available that will enable Christians to "withstand on that evil day, and having done everything, to stand firm" (Ephesians 6:13). We will also remind ourselves that God provides these same resources for us in our struggle.

FAITHFUL LIVING

A New Testament scholar has written these words about Ephesians: "The most striking feature ... seems to me to be its great courage in the face of the future. At a time when Christian communities were invisible cells in the world of their time, minority groups in the great cities of the ancient world, without any prospect of influencing the wider world or the society in which they were set ... the author of Ephesians dared to call the 'community of God' the great *universal instrument* of peace in the world."[1]

The early Christians believed that Jesus Christ came into the world at the "right time," and they also believed that the church was created by the Holy Spirit of God at the right time. The truth was so simple and yet so profound: This was the right time for the church because the world needed the church.

As it was then, so it is now: The world needs the church. Christians face resistance when they try to stand firm for God and for the best interests of the world, however. In the face of this opposition, we must recognize the enemy against which we struggle.

"For our struggle is not against enemies of blood and flesh" (Ephesians 6:12). In this passage we hear an echo of Jesus' words to Pilate: "My kingdom is not from this world. If my kingdom were from this world, my followers would be fighting to keep me from being handed over to the Jews" (John 18:36). In the Letter to the Ephesians the enemy is identified as the rulers, authorities, cosmic powers, and spiritual forces of evil (Ephesians 6:12). This enemy reveals itself in the irreligion and immorality of the surrounding culture and in the various forms that sin takes in the lives of people—be that greed, lust, anger, evil talk, gossip, envy, or any of the other evidences of "darkness" Paul identified.

It may be best to say that evil in any of these forms is simply an aspect of the lack of self-giving love. Paul chose to use the metaphor of the battlefield and the warrior to make his point. This battlefield is not on some map of historical sites; it is within us. The threat is a spiritual threat that tempts us to reject the reconciling love that God offers to us and to the world.

Think for a moment of the spiritual struggle over forgiveness. Certainly, the New Testament is in favor of forgiveness. Jesus instructed his disciples to be forgiving; and when he was asked how many times the offender should be forgiven, he replied, "seventy-seven times" (Matthew 18:21-22). Jesus was saying there is no limit on how often forgiveness should be offered because the goal is reconciliation, a goal that cannot be attained without forgiveness.

A saying in our day conveys the opposite message. Have you heard it or seen it on a bumper sticker? It goes something like this: "I don't get angry; I get even." When I have heard it used, the meaning is unmistakable: "You have harmed me in some way; and I intend to hurt you, measure for measure."

There are at least three things wrong with this grudge-holding attitude. First, it blocks any possibility for reconciliation. Second, it does not allow the offending party to move beyond his or her offense. Third, it does significant spiritual damage to the person who holds the grudge. If you have ever known someone who held a grudge or if you have felt the desire to "get even" with someone, you well know what an exhausting, wasteful effort that is. It is much better when we can release that anger and let go of the hatred we feel; for then healing can begin, and we can once again direct our lives toward creative and positive goals.

It is in such internal arenas that the struggle Paul described takes place. Great spiritual adventures happen where the eye cannot see and the ear cannot hear.

What is the most important spiritual struggle you are facing in your life?

Preparing for the Struggle

In the year 1911, the world watched the unfolding of what Roland Huntford has called the "last classic journey of terrestrial discovery."[2] The Norwegian Roald Amundsen and the Englishman Robert Falcon Scott raced across the frigid Antarctic for the honor of being the first human to set foot at the South Pole. Amundsen was successful, reaching the pole first and returning safely. Scott and many of his companions, reaching the pole later, perished on the trip back. Roland Huntford credits the better preparation of Amundsen for the former's success and the mistakes of Scott for the latter's failure. In reading the story, we discover the secret of Amundsen's preparation: He understood the hostile environment he had to overcome, he understood his own limitations and his need to rely on trustworthy companions and equipment, and he understood the resources that were available to him and used them effectively.

The Christian struggle is a journey of exploration not unlike the journey to the South Pole. Those who undertake it will need the same careful preparation Amundsen exhibited in his trek across the hostile Antarctic. In the last few verses of Ephesians, Paul wrote of the preparation the Christian needs to struggle successfully in a hostile environment.

In these verses Paul made use of the image of the warrior. We all face spiritual struggles that both challenge us and give our lives meaning. After all, adventure excites and motivates us. The Christian life is an adventure. The problems life throws our way can be understood as tests of our strength and purpose.

One of the things I learned from hiking the Grand Canyon was that the human body seems better suited to going uphill than down. While one's heart and lungs are under greater stress when going up, the legs and back seem to respond better than when going down. Perhaps God has created us to face challenges, that is, to climb uphill. So we must prepare to engage the enemy.

How do you prepare to engage in spiritual struggles?

Using Spiritual Resources

Paul reminded the church that God had already provided the resources needed in the fight against sin and evil. God has provided the spiritual resources of truth, righteousness, peace, and faith. Each of these gifts has its own importance.

For example, the truth God has revealed in Jesus Christ protects the Christian against the confusing claims of competing ideologies. Some people may be tempted, like Pilate, to ask, "What is truth?" (John 18:38). For Christians, truth is revealed in Jesus Christ. We know what God is like because of Jesus Christ; we know what God's intention is because of Jesus Christ.

Other religions and philosophies of life can teach us interesting and helpful things. For instance, Native American cultures offer an example of a positive relationship between humankind and nature that can guide us all. These other truths must be tested against the truth of Jesus Christ who gives the ultimate expression of the love of God and of neighbor, however. Jesus demonstrated that the essence of God is love. He showed that God is willing to go to any lengths to save humankind. We can wrap ourselves in this truth. Doing so will protect us from being shaken by experiences that seem to deny the loving, caring nature of God.

Likewise, the gift of true righteousness provides defense against the most insidious spiritual disease: self-righteousness. Paul urged Christians to live moral, exemplary lives. Not only should Christians refrain from the obvious immoralities of society, they should resist sins of the spirit; and they should reach out in active love toward the neighbor.

At the same time, Paul affirmed that God was the ultimate source of whatever good works we perform. That is, we have been loved by God even though we are not righteous because we need that love. Assured we are loved because of God's act in Jesus Christ, we can live the moral life to which we are called. The integrity of this moral life is the "breastplate of righteousness" (Ephesians 6:14) Paul described.

The message a reconciled people bring to the world is the gospel of peace. How is this part of our spiritual defense? Paul spoke of it as footwear. He said, "As shoes for your feet put on whatever will make you ready to proclaim the gospel of peace" (Ephesians 6:15).

Perhaps we can stretch the metaphor a bit. I find that when I take a hike, it is important that my footwear be of the right type. I happen to need a high shoe that gives added strength to my ankles. A boot with good traction is helpful on gravely trails. Here in Minnesota at certain times of the year, the "overshoe" is essential. In short, appropriate footwear is needed if you want to accomplish your purpose.

Remember how concerned Paul was about divisions in the church? The spiritual adventure of Christians includes learning to live with diverse persons within the church community.

The gospel of peace is vital as we work to be in harmony with Christ and with each other. In effect, Paul is saying that if we want to move through the terrain in which we struggle, we will need to walk in the footwear of the gospel of peace.

The fourth resource is "the shield of faith" (Ephesians 6:16). Christian faith is an abiding trust that God is working out the divine purpose. Covered by such faith, Christians are protected against both inner and outer forces that would damage the confidence we need to continue our discipleship. Martin Luther's hymn of faith "A Mighty Fortress Is Our God" is eloquent in its statement of assurance. For some reason part of the third verse has been especially easy for me to remember:

> And though this world, with
> devils filled,
> should threaten to undo us,
> we will not fear, for God has
> willed
> his truth to triumph through us.[3]

This sort of faith can be expressed even by an "ambassador in chains" (Ephesians 6:20).

Truth, righteousness, peace, faith: These are some of the spiritual resources God has provided to equip us in our struggle against the forces of evil. There may be no more "classic journeys of terrestrial discovery" left for humankind, but for each person there remains a lifelong struggle that parallels Paul's. Christian life is a great adventure in which we will find that God is trustworthy and that commitment to Christ is the source of our personal fulfillment. We cannot expect that we will never experience tragedy or encounter serious temptation or confront forces opposed to Christian faith; these are elements of our struggle. We can be assured, however, that God has already provided the resources we need to remain faithful—the resources of our hope.

ιw have the spiritual resources of truth, righteousness, peace,
faith enabled you to struggle against the forces of evil?

CLOSING PRAYER

Almighty God, giver of every good and perfect gift, we praise you for the spiritual resources you have given your children. Grant us the grace that we may accept and use your good gifts in the struggle that we face. We pray in the name of Jesus Christ, who gives us the victory. Amen.

---

[1] From *Christ,* by Edward Schillebeeckx (Crossroad, 1981); page 217.
[2] From *The Last Place on Earth,* by Roland Huntford, (Atheneum, 1986); page 497.
[3] From "A Mighty Fortress Is Our God," in *The United Methodist Hymnal* (Copyright © 1989 by The United Methodist Publishing House); 110.